BLAZERS

SUPER SPEED

DRAG Racing

BY LORI POLYDOROS

Reading Consultant:
Barbara J. Fox
Reading Specialist
Professor Emerita
North Carolina State University

Content Consultant:
Eric Lotz
Director, NHRA Field Marketing
Glendora, California

CAPSTONE PRESS
a capstone imprint

Blazers Books are published by Capstone Press,
1710 Roe Crest Drive, North Mankato, Minnesota 56003
www.capstonepub.com

Library of Congress Cataloging-in-Publication Data
Polydoros, Lori, 1968–
Drag racing / by Lori Polydoros.
   p. cm. — (Blazers. Super speed.)
   Includes bibliographical references and index.
   Summary: "Describes dragsters and drag racing, including safety features and rules governing drag
races"—Provided by publisher.
   ISBN 978-1-4296-9996-9 (library binding)
   ISBN 978-1-4765-1360-7 (ebook PDF)
   1. Drag racing—Juvenile literature. 2. Dragsters—Juvenile literature. I. Title.
GV1029.3P65 2013
   796.72—dc23   2012028360

Editorial Credits
Mari Bolte, editor; Kyle Grenz, designer; Eric Manske, production specialist

Photo Credits
Dreamstime: Amansker, 26, Gorgios, 14-15, 25 (bottom), Rozenn Leard, 7; Getty Images: Time
Life Pictures/Ralph Crane, 17; Newscom: Cal Sport Media/John Pyle, 29, Cal Sport Media/
Josh Holmberg, 18, Icon SMI CAQ/Doug James, 5, 12-13, 22, ZUMA Press/Dan Wozniak, cover;
Shutterstock: Christopher Halloran, 27, Steve Mann, 20-21, Walter G Arce, 8-9, 10-11, 25 (top)

Artistic Effects
Shutterstock: 1xpert, My Portfolio, rodho

Printed in the United States of America in Brainerd, Minnesota.
092012   006938BANGS13

TABLE OF CONTENTS

ALL ABOUT SPEED

Two race car drivers **rev** their engines. The ground shakes as the powerful cars leave the starting line. They take off faster than a fighter plane. Four to six short seconds later, the drag race is over.

rev—to make an engine run quickly and noisily

FAST FACT

A drag race track is called a drag strip. Drag strips are straight tracks and are usually 0.25 mile (0.4 kilometer) long.

MEET THE DRAGSTERS

Top fuel cars are the fastest racing machines on Earth. They race down the track at 300 miles (483 km) per hour. These lightweight cars are powered by **supercharged** engines that use special gas.

supercharged—supplied with extra energy or power; superchargers increase the pressure of the fuel and air mixture in a car's engine to increase the engine's power

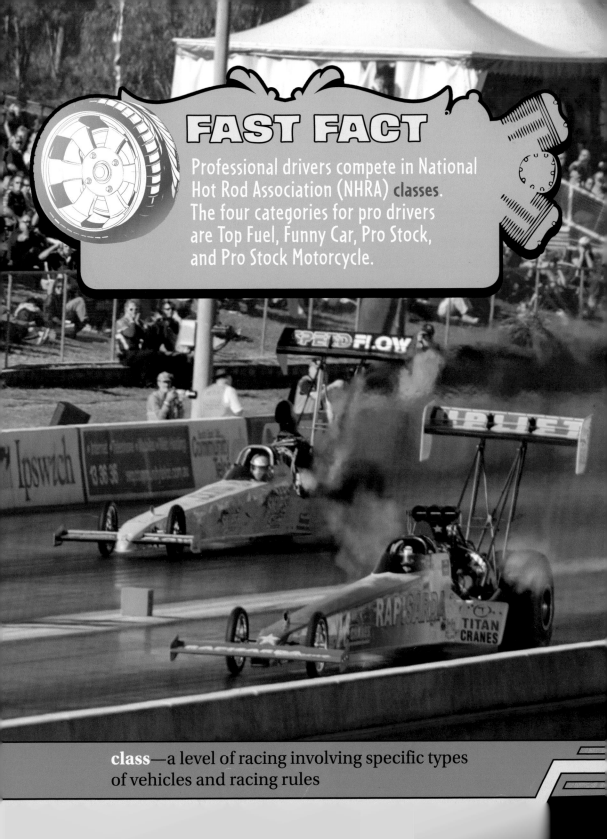

FAST FACT

Professional drivers compete in National Hot Rod Association (NHRA) classes. The four categories for pro drivers are Top Fuel, Funny Car, Pro Stock, and Pro Stock Motorcycle.

class—a level of racing involving specific types of vehicles and racing rules

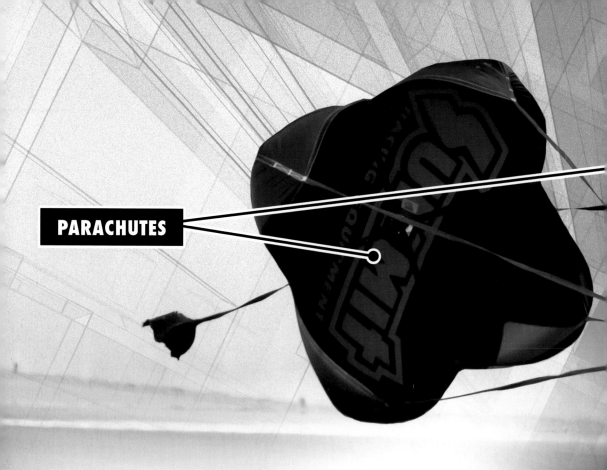

PARACHUTES

Pro stock cars look like normal cars. But these dragsters can reach speeds of 200 miles (322 km) per hour. Two **parachutes** slow down each car after the race is over.

parachute—a large piece of strong fabric that helps slow down a car

FAST FACT

The NHRA has more than 200 classes of vehicles. Things such as vehicle type, weight, and engine size decide what category a car races in.

Funny cars get their name from the funny looking changes made to them. Features such as oversized **slicks** help the cars travel faster. But high speeds combined with smooth tires also mean more danger in case of a crash.

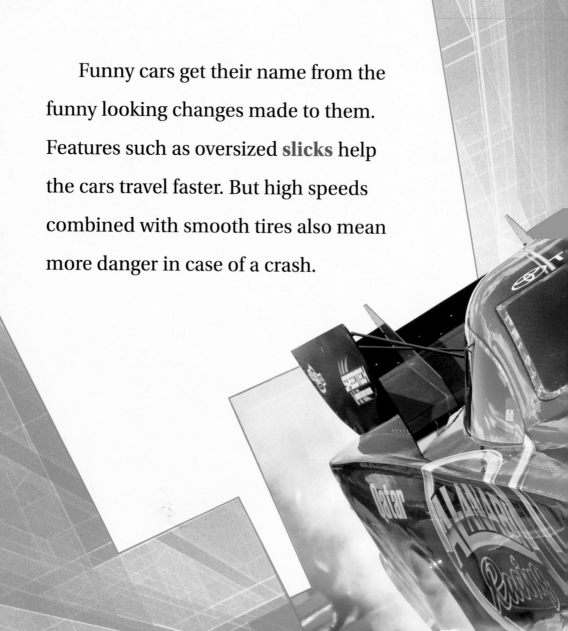

slick—a racing tire made with a smooth, soft surface to get a strong grip on the track

All pro drag racing drivers must protect themselves with safety harnesses and **fire suits.**

fire suit—a protective body suit that helps resist fire; fire suits are made with a nylonlike material called Nomex

Some riders say that riding a pro stock motorcycle is like being shot out of a cannon! These super speedy bikes hit the finish line going 195 miles (314 km) per hour. From start to finish, races can last less than seven seconds.

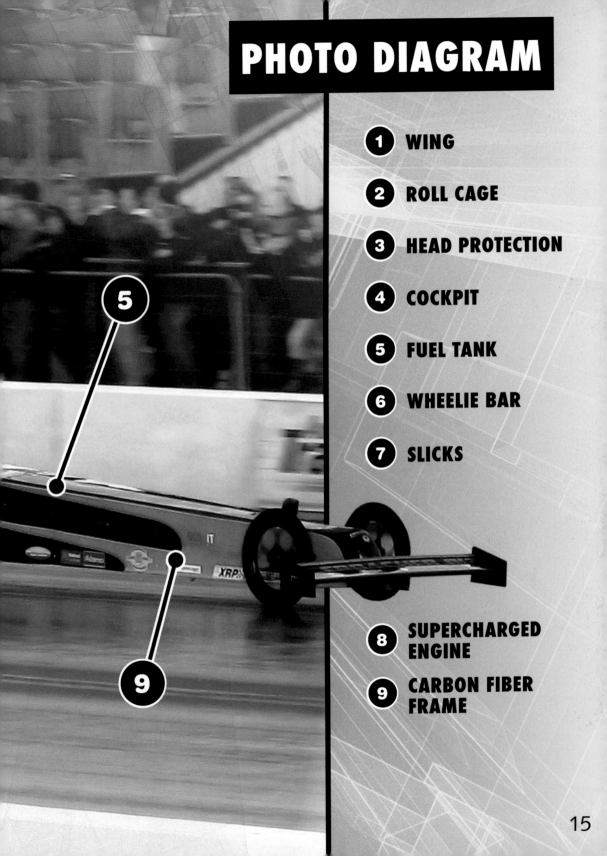

PHOTO DIAGRAM

1. **WING**
2. **ROLL CAGE**
3. **HEAD PROTECTION**
4. **COCKPIT**
5. **FUEL TANK**
6. **WHEELIE BAR**
7. **SLICKS**
8. **SUPERCHARGED ENGINE**
9. **CARBON FIBER FRAME**

NHRA RACING RULES

In the late 1940s, people began turning regular cars into **hot rods**. They raced one another in flat, open areas such as dry lake and riverbeds, country roads, and airfields. The NHRA was formed in 1951. Official rules and races were formed to keep drivers safe.

hot rod—a car that has been changed to give it extra power or speed

an NHRA race on April 1, 1957

FAST FACT

The first series of Top Fuel, Funny Car, and Pro Stock races has eight **heats**.

If you go to an NHRA race, you'll hear tires squeal and engines roar. Drivers spin their tires to perform **burnouts**. Burnouts improve the tires' grip on the track. Cars line up to compete in a series of two-car heats.

heat—one of several early races that determine which drivers advance to the feature event

burnout—the act of keeping a car in one spot while spinning the tires; burnouts heat the tires and improve their grip on the track

Lights on top of the **Christmas tree**
tell the drivers to enter the **staging area**.
Larger yellow lights mean, "get ready."
The green light means "go!"

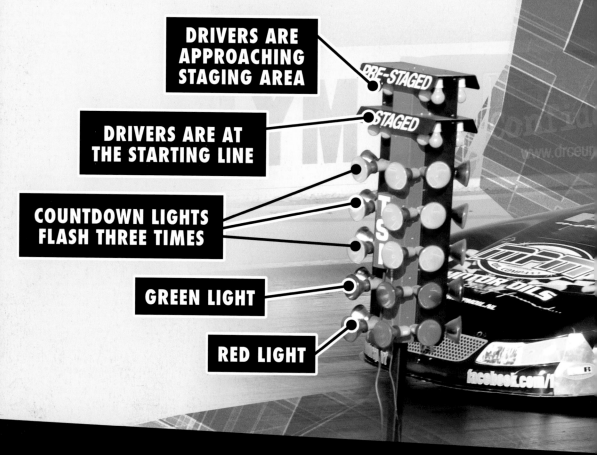

DRIVERS ARE APPROACHING STAGING AREA

DRIVERS ARE AT THE STARTING LINE

COUNTDOWN LIGHTS FLASH THREE TIMES

GREEN LIGHT

RED LIGHT

Christmas tree—the row of lights used to start a drag race

staging area—the area of the drag strip before the starting line

disqualify—to prevent someone from taking part in or winning an activity

When two cars in the same category compete, they use the heads-up racing system. This means that the first car across the finish line wins. Top Fuel, Funny Car, Pro Stock, and Pro Stock Motorcycle all use heads-up racing.

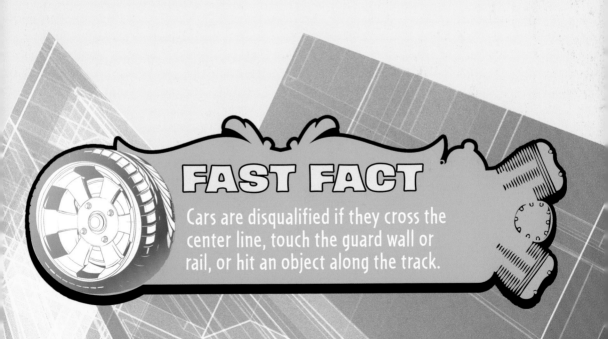

FAST FACT

Cars are disqualified if they cross the center line, touch the guard wall or rail, or hit an object along the track.

Handicap racing ensures that cars of different speeds race fairly. Drivers decide how many seconds it will take their cars to get to the finish line. The chosen time is called a dial-in. Drivers try to run as close to their dial-in time without going over.

handicap—an advantage given to a slower car to make competition more equal

The slower car is given a head start to make the race even. But what if both cars cross the finish line at the same time? The driver who reacted the fastest at the starting line and also ran under his or her dial-in time wins.

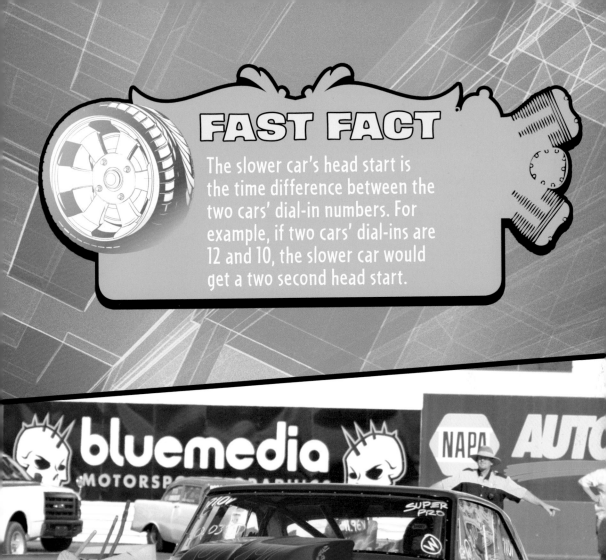

FAST FACT

The slower car's head start is the time difference between the two cars' dial-in numbers. For example, if two cars' dial-ins are 12 and 10, the slower car would get a two second head start.

RACING IN THE NHRA

The popularity of drag racing continues to grow. The NHRA is the world's largest motorsport organization. It has around 80,000 members. More than 65 million people tune in to watch NHRA races on TV every year.

FAST FACT

To compete in the NHRA, all you need is a driver's license and a car that meets safety and class rules.

GLOSSARY

burnout (BURN-owt)—the act of keeping a car in one spot while spinning the tires; burnouts heat the tires and improve their grip on the track

Christmas tree (KRISS-muhss TREE)—the row of lights used to start a drag race

class (KLASS)—a level of racing involving specific types of vehicles and racing rules

disqualify (dis-KWAHL-uh-fy)—to prevent someone from taking part in or winning an activity; competitors can be disqualified for breaking the rules of their sport

fire suit (FYR SOOT)—a protective body suit that helps resist fire; fire suits are made with a nylonlike material called Nomex

handicap (HAN-dee-kap)—an advantage given to a slower car to make competition more equal

heat (HEET)—one of several early races that determine which drivers advance to the feature event

hot rod (HOT ROD)—a car that has been changed to give it extra power or speed

parachute (PAIR-uh-shoot)—a large piece of strong fabric that flies out behind a dragster at the end of the race; the parachute helps slow down the car

rev (REV)—to make an engine run quickly and noisily

slick (SLIK)—a racing tire made with a smooth, soft surface to get a strong grip on the track

staging area (STAYJ-ing AR-ee-yah)—the area of the drag strip before the starting line

supercharged (SOO-puhr-charjd)—supplied with extra energy or power; superchargers increase the pressure of the fuel and air mixture in a car's engine to increase the engine's power

30

READ MORE

Georgiou, Tyrone. *Funny Car Dragsters.* Fast Lane. New York: Gareth Stevens Pub., 2011.

Sandler, Michael. *Dynamic Drag Racers.* Fast Rides. New York: Bearport Pub., 2011.

Von Finn, Denny. *Drag Racing Motorcycles.* The World's Fastest. Minneapolis: Bellwether Media, 2011.

INTERNET SITES

FactHound offers a safe, fun way to find Internet sites related to this book. All of the sites on FactHound have been researched by our staff.

Here's all you do:

Visit *www.facthound.com*

Type in this code: 9781429699969

 Check out projects, games and lots more at
www.capstonekids.com

INDEX